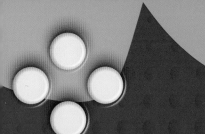

Minecraft Dungeons:

Combat

DEFEAT THE MONSTR
MACHINES

REDSTONE MONSTROSITY

T0061960

Josh Gregory

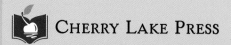
CHERRY LAKE PRESS

Published in the United States of America by Cherry Lake Publishing Group
Ann Arbor, Michigan
www.cherrylakepublishing.com

Reading Adviser: Beth Walker Gambro, MS, Ed., Reading Consultant, Yorkville, IL

Cherry Lake Press is an imprint of Cherry Lake Publishing Group.

Library of Congress Cataloging-in-Publication Data has been filed and is available at catalog.loc.gov

Cherry Lake Publishing Group would like to acknowledge the work of the Partnership for 21st Century Learning, a Network of Battelle for Kids. Please visit http://www.battelleforkids.org/networks/p21 for more information.

Printed in the United States of America
Corporate Graphics

Josh Gregory is the author of more than 200 books for kids. He has written about everything from animals to technology to history. A graduate of the University of Missouri–Columbia, he currently lives in Chicago, Illinois.

Contents

All About Action

If you've spent a lot of time playing *Minecraft*, you probably know that there is a lot of action for a game that is mostly famous for letting players build things. But even though there are plenty of enemies to battle and weapons to **craft**, combat is always pretty simple. All you really need to do is get up close and swing your sword. It's a lot of fun, but it isn't the main focus of the game.

Minecraft Dungeons is a new take on the familiar *Minecraft* world. Released in 2020, this new game focuses almost entirely on action and adventure instead of building and crafting. Most of the game is spent battling enemies. And when you aren't fighting, you'll be building up your character so you can take on more and more powerful foes.

Thankfully, the action in *Minecraft Dungeons* is a lot more interesting and complex than it was in the original *Minecraft*. There are more kinds of weapons to use, and more ways to use those weapons. There are all kinds of special abilities you can use. There is a bigger variety of enemies, each with its own unique strengths and weaknesses. Learning how all of this works can take a while, but that's all part of the fun. The more you play, the more you'll figure out how to handle different situations.

Skip

Endermen and other familiar enemies from the original *Minecraft* make a return in *Minecraft Dungeons*.

Taking Control

Depending on what kind of gaming system you're playing *Minecraft Dungeons* on, there are a few different ways to control the game. If you are on a game console, you will most likely stick to a basic controller. You'll move your character around using a thumb stick and attack by pressing buttons. If you are playing on a PC, you might prefer to use a keyboard and mouse. This can be tricky if you aren't used to it. You will use the mouse to move your character, target enemies, and attack. Keys on the keyboard will act as shortcuts to special abilities, your dodge roll, and healing. It's a lot to keep track of at first. However, once you get used to it, you'll find that a mouse lets you choose more carefully which enemies to attack at which time. Of course, it's all up to you how you want to enjoy the game. You can always use a game controller with the PC version of *Minecraft Dungeons*.

With each enemy you defeat in *Minecraft Dungeons*, you will gain experience points. Gain enough experience points, and your character's level will increase. This makes them stronger. At the same time, you'll start finding more and more powerful weapons, armor, and other gear. These items will also make your character more effective in battle. The main goal in *Minecraft Dungeons* is to keep leveling up and improving your gear until you're able to tackle any challenge in the game.

This means you won't always be moving from one dungeon to the next in order. Often, you will be replaying the same areas over and over to build up your levels and find new gear. When you replay a dungeon, you can raise the difficulty. This gives you better rewards, but it also makes the enemies even tougher.

Adjusting the difficulty of a level will give you access to all kinds of different rewards.

The bar on the bottom of the screen has everything you need to keep your character healed, dodge dangerous attacks, and use special abilities.

As you start tackling these higher difficulties, you'll notice that *Minecraft Dungeons* can be very tough. Even if you've got the right gear and you know how to play, you could get caught off guard by a tough group of enemies. Each time your character takes damage, you will lose health points. This is represented by the red heart at the bottom of the screen. If it starts to run low, you can press a button to use your red healing potion. You can see the healing potion near your health meter. Once you use it, you will need to wait some time before you use it again. This means you should save it for when you really need it. Otherwise, you might find yourself in trouble, with no way to heal when you are really in danger.

If you run out of health, your character will be knocked out and you'll lose a life. However, you'll start with full health near the point where you were knocked out. You will get three lives each time you start a new dungeon. If you lose all three, you'll be sent back to camp. You'll need to start the dungeon from the beginning.

Your health isn't the only important information shown at the bottom of the screen. You'll also see which special abilities you have and whether they are ready to use. You'll see how many arrows and emeralds you have. And you'll also see a little blue arrow. This shows whether or not you can use your dodge roll move. This move is powerful because it lets you avoid enemy attacks. But you have to wait a little while between each roll. The arrow will be blue if you can roll and gray if you cannot.

Are you ready to battle your way through the world of *Minecraft Dungeons*? Fire up the game, create your character, and let's get started!

CHAPTER 2

Doing Damage

When you create a new character in *Minecraft Dungeons*, you'll start with a simple sword. This is your first **melee** weapon. You have to get up close and personal with enemies to swing it and do damage. But, just a few minutes into the game's first level, you'll pick up a bow. This is your first ranged weapon. You can use it to attack enemies from a distance. However, you only have so many arrows. If you run out, you can't fire your ranged weapon until you find more.

Alternating between melee and ranged attacks is a big part of combat in *Minecraft Dungeons*. Some enemies are best fought with one weapon or the other. But in general, you'll want to alternate between them as you move through dungeons. You'll get a feel for when to use each type of attack as you play more and learn more about the game.

Want to know how strong your weapons are? Open up your **inventory** screen. This will show you everything you are carrying. It will also let you change which gear is currently equipped on your character. Each weapon does damage within a certain range of numbers. For example, you might have one sword that does between 30 and 49 damage and another that does between 25 and 40 damage. The higher the numbers, the more quickly that weapon can be used to defeat enemies.

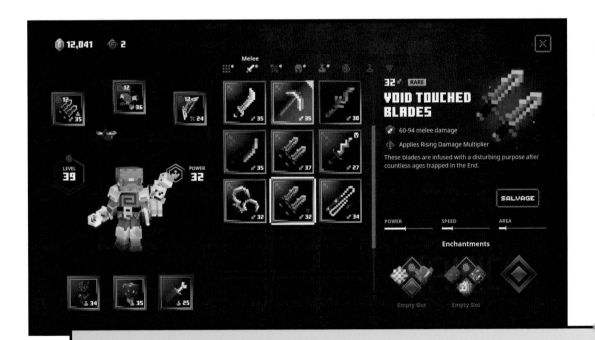

Keep a close eye on your weapon stats if you want to be effective in combat.

x3 Thorns

Some weapons, like the sickles, move extremely fast, allowing you to do a lot of damage even though each hit is somewhat weak.

Damage numbers aren't the only thing to consider when choosing which weapons to equip, though. There are all kinds of different weapons to find in *Minecraft Dungeons*. Melee weapons include swords, axes, daggers, and more. Each one feels slightly different to use. Some weapons can be swung faster than others, letting you attack more frequently. Others have a longer range, letting you hit enemies from a little farther away. Try different ones and see what feels best to you. No matter how much damage a weapon does, you won't like it if it feels clunky.

Ranged weapons come in the form of various bows and crossbows. They may all look similar, but they can attack in all kinds of different ways. Some shoot multiple arrows out in several directions when you fire them. Others launch arrows that home in on enemies even if your aim isn't perfect. And if you hold down the ranged attack button before firing, you can charge up your shot to do bonus damage. This is especially useful

Gearing Up

Keeping a close eye on your gear and always looking for upgrades are among the biggest keys to success in *Minecraft Dungeons*. No matter how much you like the gear you are using, you should always be searching for something better. This doesn't just mean more powerful weapons. You also need to upgrade your armor. This will give you additional health and protect you from taking damage from enemy attacks.

To find new gear, simply replay levels at higher difficulties. Be sure to search them carefully for hidden areas and secrets. This is often where you will find the best gear. Or, if you prefer, you can buy new things from merchants in your camp by spending emeralds.

when you are trying to take down a specific powerful enemy from a distance.

Each weapon also comes with possible enchantments you can unlock. Enchantments are special properties that make your weapon stronger. For example, one enchantment might cause a weapon to do bonus damage against a certain type of enemy. Another

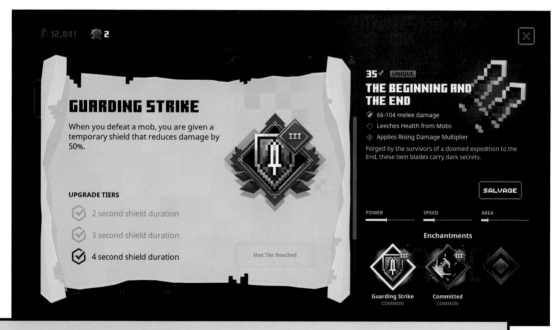

This weapon enchantment offers extra defense after defeating enemies. This makes it good for wading into big crowds of bad guys.

This weapon only has one enchantment slot, but there are three possible enchantments to choose from.

might cause enemies to take damage automatically if they get too close to you. Or it might make your attacks faster. Or it could cause your arrows to hit extra targets. There are all kinds of enchantments, and some of them are very, very powerful.

Each weapon can have up to three different enchantment slots. In each slot, you will get to choose between two or three different enchantments. But you can only choose one per slot. The number of slots and which enchantments you get to choose from are random. This means two swords of the same type can have completely different enchantments, making them very different weapons.

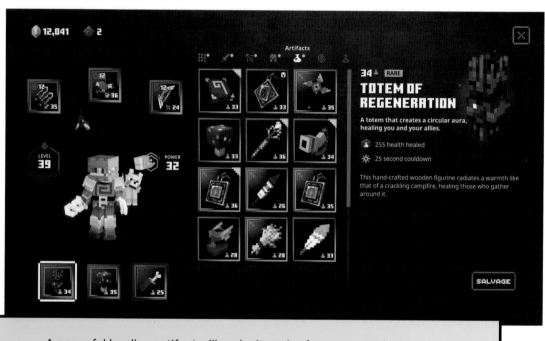

A powerful healing artifact will make it easier for you to make it through long, difficult battles.

You can unlock the enchantments on an item by spending enchantment points. You get these from leveling up. This means the higher your level, the more powerful your weapons can be. And you should spend your enchantment points freely. You can always get them back later to use on a new weapon.

Aside from your main weapons, you can also equip up to three artifacts at a time. An artifact is an item that gives your character a special ability. For example, one might push back all the enemies near you, clearing room for you to move. Another might shoot a laser beam across the screen, damaging everything in its path. Perhaps best of all, you can find artifacts that let you call pets into battle to help you. These pets can damage enemies. They are also able to distract enemies from attacking you.

Much like your dodge roll move and your healing potion, each artifact is on a timer, so you will need to wait some time for it to recharge after using it. The right combination of artifacts and enchantments can be very powerful, so experiment and see what works well together.

CHAPTER 3

Monsters and More

All kinds of dangerous enemies roam the world of *Minecraft Dungeons*. Some of them are bigger threats than others, but each one has the potential to send you to the game over screen if you aren't careful.

Each enemy type has its own strengths, weaknesses, and attack patterns. Learning how to deal with different enemy types will make it much easier to progress through dungeons and find new gear.

The most basic enemies, such as simple illagers, zombies, and skeletons won't do much more than charge toward you and attack. Some will use melee attacks while others will fire at you from a distance. These basic enemies should go down in just a couple of hits if you are keeping up with gear upgrades.

The biggest threat they present is when they show up in large numbers or alongside more dangerous foes.

There are some enemies you'll really want to watch out for. For example, creepers can ruin your day very quickly. Just like in the original *Minecraft*, these enemies will charge toward you and start flashing. After a second or two, they will explode, doing huge damage. You'll want to take them out before they have

If you see a creeper coming, take care of it as quickly as you can.

a chance to do this. Ranged attacks can really come in handy for this. They don't have a lot of health, so you should be able to handle it if you spot them quickly.

Spiders can also cause trouble. These enemies will launch webs at you. If you get it, you will be stuck in place for a few moments. This might not sound like a big deal. But if there are a lot of enemies around, they

Here, the purple beam shows that one enemy is casting a spell to strengthen another. Take out the spell caster first.

can quickly surround you and do damage while you are unable to move.

Some enemies have magical abilities. For example, you might notice an enemy shooting a magical beam toward another enemy. This is an enchanter. Enchanters use magic to make other enemies stronger. Take them out as soon as you can and the other enemies will go back to normal.

You might also run into a situation where stone pillars suddenly rise up from the ground, limiting your movement. This is a spell cast by an enemy called a geomancer. Or you might see blue flames rise up beneath your character's feet. Move away quickly, as these flames will cause damage. They are from a spell cast by an enemy called a wraith. This enemy can also **teleport** around, so targeting them can be tricky.

As you advance to later dungeons, you will start running into enemies that carry shields. You will need to destroy these before you can cause any damage to the enemy. Be careful, though. These enemies are still a threat even without their shields. If their attacks land, they will do a lot of damage.

Sometimes you will come across an especially tough enemy that gets its own health bar near the top of the screen. This is a miniboss.

Believe it or not, there are also special enemies that are even more difficult to defeat than minibosses. These unique foes are called bosses, and they show up at very specific points in the game. Usually, they are located at the end of a dungeon. In the main *Minecraft Dungeons* story, there are five different bosses.

The first boss you'll run into is the Corrupted Cauldron. This boss shows up at the end of the Soggy Swamp. At

Step into the Arena

Fairly often, you will run into situations where a magical wall or a gate suddenly springs up to block your path. Then, wave after wave of enemies will start teleporting into the area. These are called arena battles. Usually, the first wave or two will be pretty easy to clear. But as the battle goes on, each wave will get tougher. You'll need to survive each wave of enemies until the battle is finally over. Only then will you be able to proceed further into the dungeon.

first, it might seem simple to defeat. It stays in one place, and it doesn't seem to have a lot of attacks. But soon it will begin summoning purple slime cube enemies to attack you. It will also start surrounding itself with flames. Attack it from a distance, or try running into land a few hits before dodging away.

The Corrupted Cauldron can be a tough fight if you are just starting out.

Next, you'll meet the Redstone Monstrosity near the end of Fiery Forge. Watch out for lava pits in the floor as you battle this very strong enemy. Like Corrupted Cauldon, it can summon enemies to help make things harder for you. It moves very slowly, though, so run in and hit it with your most powerful attacks.

In the Desert Temple, you'll do battle with the Nameless One. This spell caster will summon skeletons

Some bosses, such as the Redstone Monstrosity, are much, much larger than regular enemies.

that carry shields. It will also shoot bursts of magic at you, and it can disappear and reappear in different places as you fight.

At the end of the game's final dungeon, the Obsidian Pinnacle, you'll face two bosses in a row. The first is the Arch-Illager himself. He has powerful magic attacks and can teleport. However, he doesn't have a lot of health. Once you defeat him, you'll have to deal with the Heart of Ender. This is the toughest boss in the main game. It will attack you with laser beams, flames, and magical orbs. You'll need to focus on dodging these attacks and deal damage only when you get a good chance. Ranged attacks are especially helpful here, as getting too close can make it harder to avoid the boss's attacks.

CHAPTER 4

Battle Strategies

If you have good equipment, very few regular enemies aren't all that tough to defeat on their own. Things only start to get tricky when they show up in certain combinations. For example, if your movement is limited by a spider or a geomancer, a wraith's spells are likely to cause more damage. Or if several creepers all show up at once, you might have trouble knocking them all out before one explodes. Or maybe a bunch of enchanters are making tough, shielded enemies even stronger, all while ranged attackers hit you from a distance. In these situations, you'll need to think carefully and quickly about which enemies to take out first and how best to do it.

It's usually best to start with the enemies that pose the greatest threat. So, for example, taking out any creepers in the room should usually be your first priority. Then you might want to focus on any enemies with the ability to limit your movement. Use ranged attacks to clear these enemies out quickly and avoid chasing them around. By now, you might be surrounded by a group of hard-hitting melee enemies. If you have the right artifacts, you might be able to push enemies back and clear a path. If not, you might need to just start swinging. Try to focus on attacking one enemy at a time until all its health is gone. Then move on to the next. If you just attack enemies at

When you are surrounded by enemies using ranged attacks, it's best to use a few ranged attacks of your own.

random, you might do a little bit of damage to many of them without knocking any out. It's more important to reduce their numbers as soon as you can.

No matter what you're up against, it's rarely a good idea to go charging into a battle without any plan. Unless you have gear that is designed to absorb a lot of damage, you might not want to rush in at all. Hang back and start with a few ranged attacks. If you are near a door or hallway, you might retreat and let

CRASH THE GATES
UNDER THE COVER OF DARKNESS

2,311

Here, the spider could freeze your character in place, leaving you open to melee attacks from the other enemies.

Retreating into empty rooms can make enemies follow you, giving you a chance to take them out one by one.

enemies come to you. This can make them more manageable. You won't get surrounded so easily. You can also use walls and other obstacles as cover from enemy ranged attacks.

Enemies will drop a variety of usable items that can quickly turn the tide in a battle. Some will drop apples, pork, and other food items. These are very useful because they can heal your character when you pick them up. Like your regular health potion, you should avoid using them until the time is right. If you just pick them up as soon as they drop, you might waste them.

You can also pick up several different kinds of potions. A strength potion makes your attacks stronger, while a swiftness potion makes you move faster. A shadow brew will turn your character invisible for a few seconds and greatly increase attack power. When you pick this up, head toward the strongest enemy and launch a surprise attack. You might even knock them out in a single hit.

Occasionally, you'll see blocks marked with the letters "TNT." These are explosives. You can pick them up and

Teaming Up

If you are playing *Minecraft Dungeons* in multiplayer with friends, there are all kinds of other combat strategies you can try. Maybe one player will focus on taking out ranged enemies while another draws the attention of melee enemies. Or maybe players will attack from different sides, surrounding groups of enemies. Talk to your teammates as you play and think about how to approach each combat situation.

You can carry two TNT boxes at a time. A well–timed explosion can help clear out a large group of enemies quickly.

carry them around. When you press the ranged attack button, your character will throw the explosive block. After a few seconds, it will blow up and do a lot of damage to any nearby enemies. This is very useful for clearing out a crowded room.

The world of *Minecraft Dungeons* can be a dangerous place. But with the right strategies, even its greatest challenges can be overcome. Keep your cool, and even if you are defeated, just keep on trying!

GLOSSARY

craft (KRAFT) to make or build something

inventory (IN-vuhn-toh-ree) a list of the items your character is carrying in a video game

melee (MAY-lay) relating to hand-to-hand combat

teleport (TEL-uh-port) to travel instantly from one place to another

FIND OUT MORE

Books

Milton, Stephanie. *Guide to Minecraft Dungeons: A Handbook for Heroes*. New York: Del Rey, 2020.

Zeiger, Jennifer. *The Making of Minecraft*. Ann Arbor, MI: Cherry Lake Publishing, 2017.

Websites

Minecraft Dungeons
https://www.minecraft.net/en-us/about-dungeons
Check out the official *Minecraft Dungeons* website for the latest updates on the game.

Minecraft Dungeons Wiki
https://minecraft.fandom.com/wiki/Minecraft_Dungeons
This fan-created wiki is packed with useful details about *Minecraft Dungeons* and its DLC.

INDEX